The Bible And The Law Of Attraction

The Bible and the Law of Attraction
© 2009 by Doron Alon
Published and distributed by: Numinosity Press Incorporated.

All rights reserved. No part of this book may be reproduced by any mechanical, photographic, or electrical process, or in the form of a recording. Nor may it be stored in a storage/retrieval system nor transmitted or otherwise be copied for private or public use-other than "fair use" as quotations in articles or reviews-without the prior written consent of the Author and Numinosity Press Incorporated. The Information in this book is solely for educational purposes and not for treatment, diagnosis or prescription of any diseases. This text is not meant to provide financial advice of any sort. The Author and the publisher are in no way liable for any misuse of the material.

Alon, Doron .
The Bible and the Law of Attraction -2nd ed ISBN: 978-0982472224
Printed in the United States of America
Book Cover Design: Created by Erin Swatzell
ginosko.designs@gmail.com

More Books By Doron: http://www.amazon.com/author/doronalon

Table Of Contents

The Bible And The Law Of Attraction

Table Of Contents

Dedication

Acknowledgments

Introduction

Chapter 1: Faith Is The Law Of Attraction

Chapter 2: Science: A Source Of Faith

Chapter 3: Feeling Are The Fuel

Chapter 4: Do You Worship The Golden Calf?

Chapter 5: Taking Action

Chapter 6: Don't Make Debt Your God

Chapter 7: What is Prosperity?

Chapter 8: Stories of Faith

Chapter 9: Showing Gratitude

Chapter 10: Prayers

Conclusion

About the Author

God is in the Whispering

Select Verses about the Law of Attraction

One Last Thing...

Dedication

I dedicate this book to the memory of my Grandmother Dorothy Meyer. I miss you more than words can express.

Acknowledgments

I would like to take this time to acknowledge the people who have helped me finish this book. I had hit many snags along the way and if it were not for their support, I would not have finished this book at all. First to my mother, she read every revision and helped me clean it up. However, most of all, her encouragement was a key to getting this book completed.

I also want to thank my dear friend Erin Swatzell for not only creating the wonderful cover for the book, but being there for me every day for months as I was going through my tough days. She kept me fired up about the book and without her help; it definitely would not have been done. I love the cover she created for this book and I hope to have many more projects for her. If you are interested in having her design a cover for you or anything that requires creative work, she can be reached at ginosko.designs@gmail.com.

I would also like to acknowledge my friends and family (they know who they are) who have always believed in me, even when I did not believe in myself. Thank you all for your support, your presence in my life has been a great gift. I want to thank God, without God, there would be nothing to cherish, nothing to love, nothing to strive for, thank you for everything.

Introduction

Thank you for buying this book, I hope it will provide you with the information you have been looking for regarding the Bible and the Law of Attraction. Surprisingly, so few books have addressed this issue directly and I am not exactly sure why. Perhaps it is because they want to distance themselves from religion. After much soul searching, I felt compelled to take it upon myself to write this book, not only to inform others but also to learn the roots of the Law of Attraction for myself in the process. While working on this book, it became clear to me that the Law of Attraction cannot be fully understood without knowing its Biblical origins.

Since the release of the best-seller 'The Secret', interest in the Law of Attraction has exploded and is increasing exponentially. With the economy spiraling downward and prospects looking bleaker and bleaker every day, many people find hope and success in life through the Law of Attraction. If you do a search online, you will find thousands of sites promising you that they have a method that will help you apply the principles of the Law of Attraction in your life. As far as I am concerned, that is wonderful. The Law of Attraction is so powerful that all these methods work.

My intention however, is to make this a quick and easy read. I intentionally kept this book short because I was noticing other books were keeping people bogged down by endless exercises, when in reality, people just want information so they can tailor it to their respective lives. Although this book does contain two or three exercises, its main purpose is to provide you with all the information you need to know about the Law of Attraction and its biblical origins. Exercises and affirmations can be very useful for some people and I have certainly attempted many of them. Nevertheless, I have found that it often becomes a deterrent; it was certainly a deterrent for me.

What you are about to read is not a method, but information about the roots of the Law of Attraction; the Biblical roots to be more specific. You will learn where in the Bible the Law of Attraction is mentioned and the core principles you need to know in order to use it. There is so much information floating around about the Law of Attraction, it is hard to make heads or tails of it all. In this book, we are going to go back to the basics. When learning about the Law of Attraction, less is more. I would like to say that I do enjoy reading the many books that are available, so you will not see me write anything negative about the other methods and teachers of the Law of Attraction; they all have something to contribute. They are all valuable and should be read as well.

For now, let us get to the root of the Law of Attraction and answer some important questions regarding it. There are a few questions I see floating around online pertaining to the Law of Attraction.

The most common one I see is:

How does the Law of Attraction apply to me if I believe in the Bible?

This is a profound question. In most of the other books about the Law of Attraction, they refer to the power that assists you in reaching your goals and desires as the "Universe". The word- universe is used to mean the underlying force of all that is, and in my estimation, a politically correct way of saying God. The term God is mostly associated with the Bible and religion in general; sadly, many people tend to be put off by the word, so universe cleverly replaces it.

However, in reality, the universe is a valid name for God. If we break down the word universe we find that it is a wonderful description of God. Uni meaning 'one' and Versus 'to turn', literally meaning "Turned into one". That one is God. God is the universe, God created the universe. If you open the Bible, it states 1 Col 1:15-17: "For by him all things were created: Things in heaven and on Earth, visible and invisible...all things were created by him and for him." In addition, Eph 4:6: "One God and Father of all, who is over all and through all and in all."

In this book, I will not use the term universe, even if the connotation is the same. I feel using the word God creates a deeper connection in our souls and makes it more personal, the word universe may not give you that feeling of closeness and connection you need to make the Law of Attraction work in your life. As you may know by now, the Law of Attraction is all about your feelings. If you do not feel it, you will not get it. Another common question I often see is:

Do we have the power and the right to ask God for anything?

The answer is yes. Two thousand years ago, Jesus was not only teaching the Law of Attraction, he was also showing us how to use it as well. In the coming chapters, I will outline some of the core references to the Law of Attraction in the Bible. Sit back, relax and enjoy.

Chapter 1: Faith Is The Law Of Attraction

The Law of Attraction is a timeless Biblical concept. Whatever you want to achieve, if you believe it can be achieved and you can see yourself as if you already have it, it will be a reality in your life. It starts as a thought and a strong desire and in time or even overnight with your faith as the fuel, God will make the desired goal manifest in your life. Although the goal may simply manifest with little or no action on your part, often you will find that God will nudge you to take the actions required that would help you reach your goals. It does not matter if the goal is a material one or not, the entire material world is created by God. Everything is a manifestation of God and nothing is too hard for God to accomplish. As the Bible states in Genesis 18:14 "is anything too hard for the Lord?"

I want to stress again that the Law of Attraction does not only apply to material goals, but also to anything you want to achieve: Inner peace, greater faith, emotional stability. It does not matter. Your faith will be the vehicle that God uses to help you achieve them. Often it can manifest in ways you could not have possibly imagined. God is funny that way, He reveals himself in ways that you could not possibly expect. This is important to keep in mind because you can often miss God's answer to your prayers because you expect it to show up in a certain way. Keep your eyes and mind open to Gods answers.

As the Law of Attraction has gained popularity through books like 'The Secret' and the works of Jerry and Esther Hicks, Joe Vitale and many others, another important question I hear people ask is about the pursuit of materialism. They question whether asking for material wealth is ungodly. Although it is true that the blind pursuit of wealth and material things is spiritually harmful, the desire for these things is not a sin nor is it wrong. If we look in the Bible, almost all the Godliest people have been wealthy.

The Bible states in Genesis 13:2 "Now Abram was very rich in live stock, in silver and gold". Abraham, who was not only an upright, faithful man, he was also a businessperson. He did not go into business to be in poverty, but to prosper, and he certainly had more than he needed to survive. God blessed him with success; God could have blessed him with just a hand-to-mouth existence, but he gave him more than he needed. Through Abraham, God has shown that abundance is not only his will for you, but also your birthright.

The following are more examples:

Both Kings David and Solomon were wealthy beyond anything that we can imagine.
In 1 Chronicles 22:14 it states of King David "...I have prepared for the house of the Lord an hundred thousand talents of Gold and a thousand thousand talents of silver and of brass and iron without weight for it is in abundance."

The Bible goes on to say of Solomon, 2 Chronicles 9:22 "Thus Solomon excelled all kings of the earth in riches and wisdom."

Joseph, who was sold into slavery by his brothers, later became the Grand Vizier of Egypt and was Pharaoh's right hand man, and acquired great wealth. His father Jacob became very wealthy working for his uncle Laban.

Genesis 30:42-43 "But when the cattle were feeble, he put them not in: so the feebler were Laban's and the stronger Jacob's. And the man increased exceedingly and had much cattle and maidservants and men servants, and camels and donkeys."

Job too was very wealthy. Job 1:3 "He possessed 7,000 sheep, 3,000 camels, 500 yoke of oxen, and 500 female donkeys, and very many servants, so that this man was the greatest of all the people of the east."

As you can see, all the above references in the Bible of these great individuals described how wealthy they were and it mentions it in a positive way, not a negative one. I can find countless other references. If you want more information about the wealthy people in the Bible, there is a series of books published on this topic, entitled The Millionaires of the Bible series, by Catherine Ponder. It is worth reading.

Please rest assured, the pursuit of material wealth is not negative, it is greed that is negative. Not all wealthy people are greedy, there are certainly very upright believers of God today who are wealthy and yet their righteousness is not called into question. If wealth is what you want, you can have it and still be a person who walks in faith. God wants you to enjoy life and prosper. We will get into much greater detail about this later in the book.

I would like to return to a previous question: Do we have the power and the right to ask God for anything?

As I mentioned in the introduction, the answer is a resounding yes! God has infused in all of us his essence and his creative power to have, be and do whatever it is that we please. Before you dismiss that, let us see what the Bible says about all this.

Let us look in the Bible and explore further, it does not matter what translation or version you have. I have used both the King James Version and New International Version's in this book. Let us dig deeper into the awe-inspiring creative energy God has instilled in you.

Let's start from the beginning.

Please open to Genesis Chapter 1:27 "So God created man in his own image, in the image of God created he him; male and female he created them" Now please go to Genesis 2:7 "and the Lord formed Man of the dust of the ground and breathed into his nostrils the breath of life and man became a living soul."

These two verses are profound and are often overlooked. However, if we look closer it tells us clearly that God has made us in His own image and likeness and that His own breath gave us life. Do you see the implications of this?

God created you not only with his own essence, but you have a portion of that creative power as well. When you breathe, that is God's breath going through your nostrils as well. God has made you in his image. Don't you think it is time we tapped into this?

Psalms 82:6 "I have said ye are Gods: and all of you are children of the most high." It is further written in 1 Corinthians 3 "know ye not...that the spirit of God dwells in you?"

God is within you and when you believe that this is true, it will activate this creative power, this creative power is the Law of Attraction. What you experience in your life is a direct result of how you use this powerful ability

God has instilled in you from creation. In fact, I often think perhaps we should rename the Law of Attraction to the Law of Creation, since in reality you are co-creating your reality, not simply attracting it to you.

Faith is the one essential element for the Law of Attraction to work in your life, faith is vital for God to give you what you strive for; faith is the key to activating the Law of Attraction. You can ask God for anything, and with faith, it will be so. Jesus was very clear about this:
Matthew 7:7 "Ask and it will be given to you; seek and you will find; knock and the door will be opened to you."

Notice that in the above verse it does not limit you to what you can ask for. God does not know limitations and neither should you. You just need to ask, and have faith that what you ask for will be given. When you establish faith, you must genuinely think differently as well, you can't simply say that you have faith. Your thinking must change. You also must be willing to take action when you get that divine nudge.

As it says in Proverbs 23:7 "It is through thinking that man forms that which he is." Once you change your thoughts, you will change your whole life. This universal truth, it cannot be denied.

Over the next few pages, I am going to show you several references to the Law of Attraction in the Bible. You will see without a doubt that God wants you to have everything you desire, all you need is faith, even a little faith will go very far.

Let's get right to it. Here are a few passages from the Bible on the Law of Attraction. Please follow along so you can read these passages with me and get excited about the potential you have and the awe-inspiring power of God, ready to manifest what you want and need most in your life.

John 14:12 "I tell you the truth, anyone who has faith in me will do what I have been doing. He will do even greater things than these."

Jesus plainly states all the great works he has done are also possible for you, all you need is faith, and you can do them, and even accomplish greater things. You cannot make this up, it is written right there.

Here are many more references to faith and its manifesting powers:

Matthew 21:22 "Whatsoever ye shall ask in prayer, BELIEVING, ye SHALL receive."

This next quote is by far my favorite one because it sums up the Law of Attraction beautifully and simply.

Mark 11:24 "What things soever ye desire, When ye pray, believe that ye receive them, and ye shall have them."

Let's break this passage down: "What things soever ye desire"-- this is a very important teaching. Jesus has just given you the right to ask for whatever you want. "Believe that ye receive them, and ye shall have them." Your job is to have faith and act as if you already have achieved your goals, and you will achieve them. This is a fundamental teaching in all the books on the Law of Attraction and Jesus said it first, two thousand years ago. In reality that quote is all you need, but I know you want to see more and luckily there are plenty more examples.
However, before I go on listing the quotes of Jesus stating how faith will manifest everything you desire. I want you to open your Bibles if you will, to the story of the Centurion. This is a magnificent story on how faith works.

Matthew 8: 5-13 "when Jesus had entered Capernaum, a centurion came to him, asking for help. "Lord," he said, "my servant lies at home paralyzed and in terrible suffering." Jesus said to him, "I will go and heal him." The centurion replied, "Lord, I do not deserve to have you come under my roof. But just say the word, and my servant will- be healed. For I myself am a man under authority, with soldiers under me. I tell this one, 'Go,' and he goes; and that one, 'Come,' and he comes. I say to my servant, 'Do this,' and he does it." When Jesus heard this, he was astonished and said to those following him, "I tell you the truth, I have not found anyone in Israel with such great faith. I say to you that many will come from the east and the west, and will take their places at the feast with Abraham, Isaac and Jacob in the kingdom of heaven. But the subjects of the kingdom will be thrown outside, into the darkness, where there will be weeping and gnashing of teeth." Then Jesus said to the centurion, "Go! It will be done just as you believed it would." And his servant was healed at that very hour."

That is powerful. A centurion, a man that was not an Israelite, and was most probably responsible for fulfilling some of the ghastly orders of Rome in his district had faith that Jesus was able to heal his servant. Jesus made it clear that it was the Centurion's faith that had healed the servant's ailment. This is an amazing story and even Jesus himself was astounded by this man's faith. You have the divine right to achieve this type of healing as well. If the Centurion, a cog in the Roman terror machine can have faith, so can you.

Here are a few more examples of how your faith is the determining factor in all manifestations in your life.

Matthew 9:20-22 " Just then a woman who had been subject to bleeding for twelve years came up behind him and touched the edge of his cloak. She said to herself, "If I only touch his cloak, I will be healed." Jesus turned and saw her. "Take heart, daughter," he said, "your faith has healed you." And the woman was healed from that moment." Once again, you can see how a person's faith will be the deciding factor. A few verses later Matthew 9:27-29 it states " As Jesus went on from there, two blind men followed him, calling out, "Have mercy on us, Son of David!" When he had gone indoors, the blind men came to him, and he asked them, "Do you believe I can do this?" "Yes, Lord," they replied. Then he touched their eyes and said, "According to your faith will it be done to you"; and their sight was restored."

The key verse here is "According to your faith will it be done to you." The above verses may be the proof you need that the Law of Attraction is from the Bible, but this is exciting, we learn by repetition and reinforcement, so I am going to supply a few more to hammer the point home.
Matthew 15:22-28 "A Canaanite woman from that vicinity came to him, crying out, "Lord, Son of David, have mercy on me! My daughter is suffering terribly from demon-possession." Jesus did not answer a word. So his disciples came to him and urged him, "Send her away, for she keeps crying out after us." He answered, "I was sent only to the lost sheep of Israel." The woman came and knelt before him. "Lord, help me!" she said. He replied, "It is not right to take the children's bread and toss it to their dogs". "Yes, Lord," she said, "but even the dogs eat the crumbs that fall from their masters' table." Then Jesus answered, "Woman, you have great faith! Your request is granted." And her daughter was healed from that very hour."

And another: Matthew 17:20 "I tell you the truth, if you have faith as small as a mustard seed, you can say to this mountain, 'Move from here to there' and it will move. Nothing will be impossible for you."

The above verse is one of the more popular verses on faith, but still people do not see the connection to the Law of attraction. That is the Law of Attraction right there, hiding in plain sight.

And more: Mark 9:23 "All things are possible to him that believe."
John 20:29 "Blessed are they that have not seen, and yet believe."
Hebrews 11:1 "Faith is the substance of things hoped for, the evidence of things not seen"

Here is another amazing quote in the Bible about asking and receiving. James 4: 2-3 "Ye Lust and have not: ye kill, and desire to have, and cannot obtain: ye fight and war, yet ye have not, because ye ask not. Ye ask and receive not because ye ask amiss."

This verse is profound, it illustrates that most or all the things that we do to receive God's blessings, most ultimately yield nothing because we do not ask correctly. We are asking amiss because we don't ask in faith. The right way is to ask, and in your asking, believe and in your believing, TAKE ACTION.

John 20:29 "Blessed are they that have not seen, and yet believe"

I know that sometimes it is hard to believe in something without concrete evidence that you can see with your eyes and touch with your hands. Many people are looking for some concrete physical signs that God is real and is active in the world.

Many well-intentioned Biblical scholars search archaeological records for such physical proof. I have read a lot about Biblical Archeology and the attempts to find that one piece of evidence; nevertheless, I realized it is not worth waiting for archeology to find physical evidence to prove anything about the Bible. Over the years, I have learned that Archeology, especially Biblical Archeology is a political field. It is often focused on the squabbles between archeologists than the underlying discoveries. This may seem like a harsh indictment of the field, but it is true. I do think Archeology is important to place certain events in their proper historical context but should not be a platform to push an ideology.

However, I feel that when it comes to the archeology that touches on Biblically related events, it is mired in politics. Understandably so, the modern world's foundation is based on western religious ideals, which if shaken, can cause massive global upheaval.

In Israel, where much of the Biblical Archeology is taking place, the Biblical Archeology "business" is run by some secular and some rather extreme religious elements. Many of the secular scholars insist that many of the archeological findings that prove the Bible to be genuine are fraudulent, betraying their bias. However, on the other hand, the religious contingent considers all artifacts that confirm their beliefs as always being authentic, not even considering the possibility that the artifact is a fraud. Sadly, there are many fraudulent pieces floating around, so a careful analysis must be done. With all this fighting between the various 'special interest groups', Biblical Archeology is biased and unbalanced and will remain so until they discover the mother load of all findings, which is yet to happen.

The leading archaeological authority in Israel is slow and hesitant to outwardly authenticate religious artifacts confirming the accuracy or validity of any New or Old Testament findings; they do this for many reasons, mostly because of religious and political pressures.
Politically speaking, what do you suppose would happen if an artifact confirming the authenticity of Jesus would have on Israel and its mostly Jewish population? I will tell you this, there will not be a mass conversion, of that I can assure you. But a massive intellectual upheaval, which may not be the worst that could happen, but pressures from those who want to maintain the status quo, will not let that happen. There is simply too much to lose, but in reality more is lost when discoveries are simply swept under

the carpet. For all we know, they may have found that one piece of evidence and they are not sharing it with the world.

What I just said was not mere conspiratorial thinking. When the Dead Sea Scrolls where discovered, many in the archeological community wanted to suppress it because of its religious implications and they almost succeeded. I would not be surprised if there are findings that are currently being suppressed. As interesting as it might be to explore Biblical Archeology, the only concrete evidence you need is when you see God working in your life.

You will be the living proof, and no one can prove such experiences of God to be fraudulent, no matter what they say or how hard they try.

Let's continue where we left off: Another question I often see asked on the Law of Attraction is:
How long will this take?

I suppose the best example I can find to explain how time works with the Law of Attraction is the work of the farmer. When a farmer sows the seeds for his crop, does he expect to reap the next day? No, of course not, he must wait and be patient. It is not that God cannot make it happen the next day, but rather it's the time in between the sowing and the reaping which allows for the various elements to fall into place so the crop can fully mature.

Being prosperous is the same thing, it is about sowing fundamental changes in your mind and letting them grow and reaping the rewards in time. You need to prepare to reap. Most of the issues in your life did not appear overnight and thus they need some time to heal. Just as a farmer during the time he sows until the time he reaps is constantly tending to that crop. So too when you sow your faith, you should be tending to your mind and soul, preparing to reap, otherwise you will not have a healthy crop. For example: Let's say you are not very good with money and you happen to win the lottery tomorrow and do not know how to invest it, what will happen? It will be gone, the same for your health and just about everything else in your life. You must prepare, but you also must have patience. Patience is a virtue that not many of us have, including myself. Nevertheless, in developing patience, you are developing a trait that will serve you in every aspect of life, not just your pursuit of prosperity. So keep working on it, I know I am, daily.

Chapter 2: Science: A Source Of Faith

I was raised to believe that a person should never talk about politics and religion. You can add science to that list as well, quite a bit of controversy has plagued the religious and scientific communities over how science fits in with religion and vise versa. Many books have been written trying to bridge the gap. I am going to take another route; I will not go into the deeper details of how Science proves God's existence, nor will I give a philosophical reason on how to bridge the gap; that would be for two separate books altogether. However, I will discuss briefly, why I believe Science is one of the most powerful vehicles to increase your faith so you can better your life.

Most people consider science as separate from religion. This is because the two factions; one being the religious community and the second being the scientific community are getting confused about the true implications of science.
The religious side contends that God created everything and that is the 'why' and the 'how' of everything...end of story. I can't argue with the fact that God created everything, I agree with that. But looking at your body, you can see there is more complexity than what is written in the Bible. The Bible was not meant to be a book of science, but a book of faith and a guide to ethical living.

The scientific side contends that the processes that are going on can easily be explained by scientific discoveries and that God is not behind them. Ah, but there is the rub, just because we have discovered the machinery behind certain processes, does not prove there isn't a God behind them, if anything, science is unveiling God's handy work. Science is a different way for us to get a glimpse at God's creative power. It should bring us a sense of awe for God's creation and not cause us to draw battle lines over it. If you look at the composition of our bodies, we have many of the same elements the earth has, we are mostly made of water just as the earth is, this confirms not only the religious perspective of being created from the dust of the earth, but this also confirms the scientific claim that we emerged from the earth and water as well. It's just another way of saying the same thing.

Evolution and Genesis:

This might get me into a little trouble with both communities here but I am going to say it. The Bible and evolution are saying the same thing.

Science tells us that first, there was nothing and then BANG, the universe came into existence. The Bible has hinted to this as well. In Genesis 1:3, it states, "let there be light, and there was light". What is that light? It was created on the first day of creation. It certainly was not the sun; the sun was not created until the fourth day. That light, I believe is the big bang. That divine moment of creation. In addition, notice all of creation- was created BEFORE humans arrived. Notice God also states that man was created from the dust of the earth (Genesis 2:7). This means the material of our bodies is from the earth and that animals were created first, not unlike what the scientific community is saying.

Whether the scientific community admits it or not, the complexity that surrounds us is awe-inspiring and at least in my mind, proves that God exists. If you want to see what I mean, go to any search engine and look up how your organs work, search for images of cells under an electron microscope, read about your brain. You will see that it is very complex and extremely organized. Something that complex could not be a result of random chance; it is too specific and too exacting to be random. Is the feeling of love just a random occurrence? Science contends that because of certain chemical reactions in the brain, the feeling of love is felt, even if this process is correct, isn't that just amazing how God purposely created us to be this way? I think the complexity of nature and how it has evolved in time is more of a miracle than just creating it out of thin air; it takes an infinite amount of intelligence and attention to detail to create all this. The sheer complexity of it all is testament to God's unfathomable power. We should be using science to uplift our faith in God, just look around you, so much proof exists. God is smiling back at us through science.

Whether the scientists admit or deny the existence of God shouldn't matter to us anyway, you can still use science as a source of faith and for practical use. Many people who create medicines for our well-being are atheists; do we boycott the medical industry and the pharmacies when we get sick? No, we wait in line to fill our prescriptions.

We should not care whether the pharmacist or the researchers believe or not, we still use their products and can still benefit from them. We need to approach scientific discoveries with that- mindset. Now the Scientists need to recognize that science only answers the "how" questions, but never the "why" questions. Science gives us quantitative reasons, religion gives us qualitative reasons. We need them both.

I read a wonderful quote by Paul H. Carr that summarizes what I just said succinctly: **"Science is an effort to understand creation. Biblical religion involves our relation to the creator. Since we can learn about the Creator from his creation, religion can learn from science."**

I could not have said it better myself. So please remain open to the discoveries of science, those discoveries are an ongoing revelation from God and can be used to INCREASE your faith.

The branch of science that studies the brain (Neuroscience) is to me the most fascinating. It is making great strides in our understanding of how thoughts influence our world. Even the most atheistic of neuroscientists can't ignore that there appears to be a "ghost in the machine", whether they call it a soul or an emergent quality of the brain, the fact remains, there is something mysterious running the show. This "mystery" and how we use it through our feelings can change our whole life and affects everything around us. We can use science as a tool, not as a weapon.

Chapter 3: Feeling Are The Fuel

I would like to make a few observations about feelings and how they create your reality. It has been scientifically proven that how you are mentally feeling has a tremendous influence on your body and your life. It is a fact that stressful thoughts can cause your body to break down. This is a fact; worry causes ulcers, heart attacks, and cancer. You name it, it can cause it. This alone is plenty of proof that thoughts, although unseen, influence what is seen. People who have positive thoughts have fewer negative physiological and psychological problems. Have you ever seen a person who feels mentally well look physically well? They have a "GLOW" to them.

 Have you ever seen yourself on the days you felt good and the days you felt bad? It's a huge difference isn't it? Your feelings are your lenses to the world. When you feel bad, you look in the mirror and say "I am fat", "I am stupid", "No one will love me because I am not worthy of love", "everything goes horribly for me", "The world is going to hell in a hand basket." We do not cut ourselves any slack on those days. What does that negative outlook look like in the mirror?

 You were probably slouching, you had bags under your eyes, and you had various aches and pains… I could go on. But when you feel good, notice that you are probably standing straight, you have a "glow". That nagging pain seems to have gone away, people notice you more. It's amazing. As the Bible states: Proverbs 23:7 "It is through thinking that man forms that which he is."

John Milton further captured this truth when he wrote, **"The mind is its own place and in itself, can make a Heaven of Hell, a Hell of Heaven."**

My final observation on feelings and thoughts is one that deals with the magnetic power these thoughts have and that if these thoughts are not properly guided, can spiral out of control and through the Law of Attraction, create circumstances that are more negative. To illustrate what I mean, let me tell you about my personal experience with magnetic thoughts and how I was using the Law of Attraction against myself and not realizing it.

In the mid 90s, I was in a serious relationship; I was living in Israel at the time. I was engaged, I had money, things could not have been better. Unexpectedly my fiancé broke up with me. I was so depressed; truthfully, I contemplated suicide. It was a very bad time for me. I could not let it go; negative thoughts started piling one on top of the other, attracting each other like a magnet. My mind was a magnet and the negative events were like iron shavings, clinging tightly to me. Within 3 months, I was broke mentally, financially and spiritually. They shut off my phone and electricity; this was the dead of winter by the way. Luckily, Israel does not get winters as we do here in the Northeastern parts of the United States, but it was still cold, the apartment I was living in did not have central heating. My bones ached almost as much as my soul.

I had just enough money to pack my things and get on a plane with my dogs and go back home to New York. I left behind debts and bad feelings. But my worries didn't end there; I had debts here as well, which I was managing until I lost it all. So I was going into serious default here. I felt horrible, and was about to feel even worse. I suddenly developed chronic and often debilitating pains, I went to many doctors at a hospital that took patients on a sliding scale since I did not have insurance, none of them knew what was wrong, and they put me on medication for almost 3 years, thinking it was some mystery condition.

I was poked and prodded, had x-rays and MRI's taken, and yet they found nothing. One doctor told me that I would just have to deal with the pains for the rest of my life, I was in my 20s, and this was a life-destroying prospect for me.

Meanwhile, the creditors did not go away, they were writing letter after letter threatening to take everything I had left. I had marshal notices threatening seizure any personal belongings I had. It was so bad I couldn't put any spare money I had in the bank in fear of the creditors taking it, which happened a few weeks earlier. Some of that money was not even mine. I eventually had to file for bankruptcy. My utility bills where being paid by my mother and sister. I often had to decide whether I would eat or my dogs would. In fact, I even stole a bag of dog food from a neighbor; it was a very bad time. One of my dogs got dangerously low in weight and although now he is fat, he still eats his food as if he was starving, and this is over 14 years later. During that time the dogs hardly went out, it was so bad that if the Department of Health ever saw how I lived they- would have condemned my apartment and would have taken away my dogs.

It was such a dark time for me. Being naturally introverted, I was also becoming reclusive as well. Just writing this made me have to take a deep breath because it was just too overwhelming.

As I stated earlier, I eventually had to declare bankruptcy and any relationships I had or formed with women were seriously dysfunctional. I was so fatigued I took over-the-counter uppers, specifically ephedrine to get me through my day; which eventually caused a horrible cycle of panic attacks, so bad in fact, I had gone to the emergency room a few times thinking I was having a heart attack.

It just spiraled into sheer darkness. One day when I could no longer take the pain, I cried and prayed to God asking for relief; this was the first time I prayed with so much feeling and power in my life, it was also the first time I encountered the Law of Attraction on a conscious level. Well, it worked; I started feeling strong in my faith that God would turn things around. Suddenly things started happening, but truly measurable things, miracles if you will. My hair stands on end just thinking about this. I met a woman who completely changed my life and took care of my dogs and got me to clean my house and redo it, she actually paid for it too.

I eventually got a job that provided me with much needed medical insurance to get a doctor I could trust. When I found the right doctor (who is still my primary care practitioner), he looked at my issues and said it was all mental. I went to therapy, used something called Switchwords and continued to enrich my spiritual life and suddenly all the pains stopped, the panic attacks gone, never to return.

That relationship eventually ended after the apartment was redone. She was an Angel sent by God to help me get on my feet. The job I had then was a retail job, it was not much money, but it was enough to push me forward and pay her back over time. Until this day, I am incredibly thankful to the managers for hiring me; it forced me to reverse the reclusive path I was on. From that moment on, life started looking up, and although I have hit rough spots along the way, we always do so we can grow. My faith in God has kept me on the right path. My life is so different now I am still in awe. God works through faith, there is no doubt at all in my mind about that.

What I am hoping to illustrate by retelling my experiences is how your feelings, if not guided with faith will spiral out of control and manifest negative situations in your life. The above story was just a short version of my experiences with faith and its power. You probably have your own stories of faith and triumph as well.

If you get anything out of this chapter, I am hoping it is that no matter how bleak you may think things are, it does not have to be this way, it can change, and it will change, just have faith that it can. As of the time of this writing (2009), the world is experiencing a collective economic and psychological depression. Now is the time to lift out of despair and let God in, frankly it is our only hope. We need to let go and let God and destroy our constant worshipping of doubt, which I call the Golden Calf. I will cover that in the next chapter.

"Life reflects your own thoughts back to you."—Napoleon Hill
"Happiness is something that you are and it comes from the way you think." --- Dr. Wayne Dyer

Chapter 4: Do You Worship The Golden Calf?

Exodus 32:1-5: 1 "When the people saw that Moses was so long in coming down from the mountain, they gathered around Aaron and said, "Come, make us gods who will go before us. As for this fellow Moses who brought us up out of Egypt, we don't know what has happened to him." 2 Aaron answered them, "Take off the gold earrings that your wives, your sons and your daughters are wearing, and bring them to me." 3 So all the people took off their earrings and brought them to Aaron. 4 He took what they handed him and made it into an idol cast in the shape of a calf, fashioning it with a tool. Then they said, "These are your gods, O Israel, who brought you up out of Egypt." 5 When Aaron saw this, he built an altar in front of the calf and announced, "Tomorrow there will be a festival to the LORD." 6 So the next day the people rose early and sacrificed burnt offerings and presented fellowship offerings. Afterward they sat down to eat and drink and got up to indulge in revelry."

This is a powerful story; it illustrates how the nation of Israel backslides as Moses was getting the 10 Commandments from Mount Sinai. However, this story illustrates something much more profound for all of us, and that is the incredibly destructive power of doubt. Doubt is the opposite of faith; doubt is an idol that we worship when we have abandoned faith. Doubt is the god we build a Golden Calf for. Think about the story of the Israelites for a moment. After everything that God had done for them; from taking them out of Egypt, to smiting the Egyptians yet sparing them. God split the sea and all of these amazing things, yet they still doubted anyway. Sound familiar? Has that ever happened to you? Have you seen God's hand obviously provide for you and yet at some point you forgot about that?

Don't beat yourself up; it happens to all of us. I used to have so much doubt; I could have been the poster boy for doubt, with a huge Golden Calf behind me. I am often in awe of how easy it is for faith to fly right out the window when times get tough. We suddenly forget that God delivered us when we had challenges in the past.

What prevents us from achieving everything we can as well as causing our prayers from being seemingly unanswered is this idol of doubt, our personal Golden Calf. When you doubt, the mind is in turmoil, you are frozen solid. But we must remember, God is always there to answer our prayers, but it is we who stumble around blinded by the Golden Calf we have created.

The great Christian monk Meister Eckhart said it best "God is at home, it is we who have gone out for a walk"

When you lose faith, you suddenly feel unsure about everything. This insecurity is a Golden Calf, and every time we have thoughts of doubt and fear, we are sacrificing ourselves and building a Golden Calf and ultimately the result is sorrow. It is not as much a punishment for worshipping the Golden Calf, as it is an effect of shifting your focus from faith to the dangerous forces of doubt and fear. Doubt is not only doubt in God but also doubt in your self-image, which is the image of God as it states in Genesis.

If we have a positive self-image, doubt has no power over us. I learned this the hard way. I have had moments in my life when I had a very poor self-image, and I do not mean just physical self-image but mental, intellectual and spiritual. I believed I was too stupid and lacked any discipline in my life. When I saw the results of my life, it just confirmed my feelings of inferiority, lack and faithlessness. It's a dark place to be in.

In time, I realized that my past performance is not indicative of my future results. We have all improved in our lives whether we see it or not. Even if you are in a bad place right now, imagine the issues that bothered you when you were younger or perhaps recently that you have long forgotten.

Have you not grown since that time? Do you still get upset over the same things you did when you were a child? The answer would probably be no. You have changed; in fact, look around you, everything in this great universe changes constantly. Nothing is static.
God has made it this way so we can learn and grow. God constantly tries to wake us up from our doubt-filled slumber but we resist waking up, constantly hitting the snooze button of life. One day when we go to hit that button, we will be 30, 40 or 50 years older and wonder where the time has gone. Change is God's wake up call to grow. It's horribly ironic that we live in a world where change is the rule and yet we are so resistant to it. We make ourselves incompatible with the world and with spirit when we resist change. This resistance to change is common, but it is not because we are incompatible, it is because we have doubt in God, doubt in our future, doubt in ourselves. I recall an e-mail I sent to a friend about this, the following paragraphs are excerpts from that e-mail, and I believe it will be of great use to present it here.

The only way to destroy that Golden Calf when you are faced with challenges and don't know where to go, is to let go and let God. The Golden Calf is alluring, it's tangible, you can feel it. Faith on the other hand seems less tangible it requires well…faith. We need to develop faith in faith itself, follow me?

It's like what the man who wanted his child healed said to Jesus in the Bible "Lord, I believe, help thou mine unbelief" in Mark Chapter 9. We have faith but need help sustaining it.
We have all seen miracles in our lives, and in fact, they are occurring everyday, right before our eyes. But for some reason we forget or we are blinded by doubt. Having doubt is a sin against ourselves because the

horrible effects it produces in our lives when we have it. In many ways, I have come to discover that it is not only our fault. We must factor in how we were raised, the environment we live in. These factors shape our conception of the world as well. Our memory records everything that has happened to us, it can have problems retrieving it at times, but it is always there and is buried alive, but it never dies, it is latent only to arise at the worst possible time. So although it is not completely our fault, it is our responsibility to change it. In order to do that we must stop blaming our parents for the way they raised us, they were doing the best they could. All blame in general must cease. Besides, that's in the past, what counts is this moment.

When we experience more negative events than positive ones, that is what eventually takes hold in our mind. We tend to take the good events for granted and the bad events to heart. It takes letting go to change that habit. It took me almost an entire lifetime to understand this. Not by affirming it was so, although that can work for some negative events, but by realizing God has a higher purpose.

This is important; you need to remember that with every hardship comes an opportunity to learn. You must also know in your heart that there is a "divine lining" to all events so to speak, knowing this helps in the process of letting go.

To get rid of the Golden Calf or at least quiet it, you must have faith and know ahead of time that there is a divine purpose. You don't have to know what that purpose is just yet, but know there is one. You should wake up every morning and give it all to God; I mean it, from the cells in your body to your soul. I started doing this every morning when I simply realized I don't know the big picture yet. But I know there is one, and that I accept anything that happens. I also mention what I want to achieve in that Morning Prayer or letting go session, as I like to call it.

In the end, by letting go you realize God will determine the best possible outcome for you. Letting go can be challenging, but it is possible.

When we hook our attention to our issues and frustrations it makes them worse, we lay our souls down to be sacrificed on the altar of the Golden Calf. Have you ever had physical pain that just got worse when you kept on thinking about it?

Why does it seem that when we are distracted we don't notice the pain or our mental state? That is because we let go of the issue and place our minds on something else. When we let go and let God, we place our attention on God. You may have heard this phrase before and it is true "Energy flows were attention goes."

However, you must open yourself up to divine flow. You can't have a conversation with another person if they do not respond in someway right? It's a 2-way conversation. The same goes when we speak to God, if you want to talk with God, you have to let go first. The hooking of your attention on the pain and frustration creates a busy signal for divine energy because you are focusing away from God. God has the ultimate switchboard; He accepts all calls and never has technical difficulties. But you need to free your line. Before a doctor can help you, you need to take the first step and go get treatment. That means letting go of you stubbornness.

Often I am asked if letting go and living in the moment are the same and why it is so hard to live in the moment and let go. Letting go and living in the moment are the same and the reason it seldom works is because people are striving to let go and striving to live in the moment. The moment you strive, you are not letting go, that is because there is a perception that "living in the moment" is supposed to feel like something. It's not supposed to feel like anything, it's a state, a mindset. You will just know when you are in that state. This is why the practice of "living in the now" is lost on many people. Sure, they read it and like the idea of it, but they think by living in the moment it is a counteraction to living in the past, future or striving in the present. It is not an action, but a state.

Letting go is having an intrinsic knowing that it is all a divine plan. When you feel tension, frustration or anger realize this is part of a divine plan and take a moment and ask God to lift it from you and help you learn a lesson and then just leave it alone.

No one said that God's plan won't be painful for you sometimes. Pain is the ultimate messenger of God's love. Knowing it is a divine plan makes it so much easier. Eventually in time, nothing will bother you anymore. With this realization, you can reframe every perceived negative event in your life as a potential opportunity to grow. You can experience joy when you encounter adversity. I know this is hard, I certainly find it difficult, but in reality, all adversity is for your betterment. That, I assure you is not a platitude, but the truth.

In James Chapter 1: 2-4 it states "Consider it all joy, my brethren, when you encounter various trials, knowing that the testing of your faith produces endurance. And let endurance have its perfect result, so that you may be perfect and complete, lacking in nothing." He is stating in no uncertain terms that adversity can be a very good thing. You just have to reframe your thinking and let go and let God.

Do you remember when Jesus was with his disciples before he was to be captured and later crucified? What did he say when he prayed? What did he do? Open to Matthew 26:39, let's read it together " And he went a little further, and fell on His face and prayed, saying, "My Father, if it is possible, let this cup pass from me; Yet not as I will, But as you will" Jesus let go and let God.

Another point id like to make on conquering the Golden Calf is it takes insight not to make everything that happens in your life about you. We are all connected. The other day a person was annoying me at work, it is not what he said nor was his behavior aimed at me, in fact, it had nothing to do with me, but it had to do with the flow of work I needed to get myself into. I am still doing my work regardless of his pace and the work will be done, but he would be wrapped up in a book when he should clearly be doing work that would help us all leave a bit earlier than usual. I looked forward to leaving early because I needed to get sleep since I had to work early the next day

. At first, I felt angry thinking, "What is wrong with this guy? Why is he so darn slow and easily distracted?" Then I let it go and suddenly I thought clearly. I recall saying to myself " You do not know why he is this way, for all you know he could have had trauma and needs to escape, maybe he is in pain and unable to do the work, this guy doesn't know you need to get home to get sleep because you work the next day and it is not his problem, this is his only job and he is not here for you." When I heard this in my mind I felt compassion and realized, its okay, an extra 10 minutes won't kill me and well honestly, I did not go right to bed anyway. It is all a divine plan. I was taught patience and I was humbled.

Now the question is, how do you shift your consciousness away from the Golden Calf and on to God? This is going to sound simple and it is. I know I said I am not a big fan of exercises, but I promise this will be one of the only two or three:

Write down every time God has worked a miracle for you. Write your list and try to recall it all; from the spiritual to the material miracles. Look it over and ask yourself was this Gods work? The answer would be obvious. Does God perform miracles for me? The answer would be yes there as well. Then ask yourself, why is it that I lapse in faith? Ask it while you look over the list and that feeling you get when you do this will be a catalyst for helping you change your consciousness. It will give you a huge boost in your faith and energy. Keep this list in your pocket. Those moments that you feel your mind is becoming fodder for the sacrificial flames of the Golden Calf, feel the list in your pocket, or look it at and I have a feeling that will help you shift your focus. I have my list right here. God bless.

Chapter 5: Taking Action

The Law of Attraction is very comprehensive, not only does it require you to have faith that you can achieve whatever it is you desire, it also requires that you take action as well. It works on you spiritually, physically and mentally. You will find that once your goal is clearly stated, God will nudge you to take action. It may come as an idea or a quick realization, it could be very subtle and if you do not stay mindful, you may miss it. In fact, this chapter was written because of one of those nudges, I will explain this a bit later in the chapter. First, I want to address why God nudges you to take action rather than just telling you directly with words.

Whenever I experienced adversity, I always asked God for a direct sign as to what I needed to do to get out of it. I practically demanded that I would get it in words. I didn't have time to waste on events I could interpret a million ways. I wanted to know right now and clearly.
Although God could do that, but in reality, words are the least effective way to get one to take action. I know you may have heard that before and perhaps you questioned the validity of that statement. After all, words do convey quite a bit and they can be rather direct.

But here is why they are not effective. Have you ever heard your own thoughts in your mind? I don't mean hearing voices per se, although that can be possible, but more like direct words as to what to do? If so, have you ever doubted them? Have you ever followed them only to realize it was probably your imagination speaking? I know I have experienced that and so have many people. After a few of these, you start doubting your own inner dialogue. You simply do not trust the words generated in your mind because they have let you down. With this in mind, how would you know if it was God talking to you or not? If you doubt the words, chances are you would doubt them no matter where they come from. Now let's look at synchronistic events for a moment. Have you ever experienced an event that was so coincidental that it simply shocked you? You could not imagine how something so rare and coincidental could take place. Do you trust those events?

If you think about it, statistically these events should never have happened in the first place. Those signs my friend, are clearly from God. So real that they cannot be denied like the idle chatter in the mind can be. More often than not, those events were the exact events that had to take place for you to take action. However, in order to see these events, we must remain open to them.

God has his entire creation at his disposal to make these events a reality. Your nudge may come in many different forms, but they won't just be any event, you will know when God is speaking to you through that event. Some of these events may require you to take a little risk, but risk is often a good thing when God nudges you to take them.

The idea for this chapter came after I stumbled upon the Parable of the Talents in Matthew Chapter 25. Let's read that together on the following page since it requires more space:

Matthew 25: 14-29: "For it is just like a man about to go on a journey, who called his own slaves and entrusted his possessions to them. "To one he gave five talents, to another, two, and to another, one, each according to his own ability; and he went on his journey. "Immediately the one who had received the five talents went and traded with them, and gained five more talents. "In the same manner the one who had received the two talents gained two more. "But he who received the one talent went away, and dug a hole in the ground and hid his master's money. "Now after a long time the master of those slaves came and settled accounts with them. "The one who had received the five talents came up and brought five more talents, saying, 'Master, you entrusted five talents to me. See, I have gained five more talents.' "His master said to him, 'Well done, good and faithful slave. You were faithful with a few things, I will put you in charge of many things; enter into the joy of your master.' "Also the one who had received the two talents came up and said, 'Master, you entrusted two talents to me. See, I have gained two more talents.' "His master said to him, 'Well done, good and faithful slave. You were faithful with a few things, I will put you in charge of many things; enter into the joy of your master.' "And the one also who had received the one talent came up and said, 'Master, I knew you to be a hard man, reaping where you did not sow and gathering where you scattered no seed. 'And I was afraid, and went away and hid your talent in the ground. See, you have what is yours.' "But his master answered and said to him, 'you wicked, lazy slave, you knew that I reap where I did not sow and gather where I scattered no seed. 'Then you ought to have put my money in the bank, and on my arrival I would have received my money back with interest. 'Therefore take away the talent from him, and give it to the one who has the ten talents.' "For to everyone who has, more shall be given, and he will have an abundance; but from the one who does not have, even what he does have shall be taken away"

This is an amazing parable because it illustrates the importance of taking action. In order to make this easier, try to think of the "talents" as literally your talents and abilities, the things you love to do, that you know you are good at, even if nobody else thinks so. Something that gives you joy. That talent and the joy you feel are innate God given gifts. When God gave you these gifts he expected you to make them grow because he knows if you love doing it, you will do it more and your joy will multiply abundantly. But if you do not use it, you lose it. It's not unlike your mind and your body; if you don't use them, you lose them.

This is what Jesus meant when he said, "For to everyone who has, more shall be given, and he will have an abundance; but from the one who does not have, even what he does have shall be taken away" This means if you do not invest the talents that God gives you and take action, you essentially have nothing and whatever you have will be taken from you.

Now before you dismiss that as being perhaps overly cruel or harsh think about this for a moment. Have you ever given up on something you loved for a job or situation that gave you less joy? Were you stuck in that situation? As time past, did your desire for the things you love seem to fade away? This is what is meant by "even what he does have will be taken away". Your desire for what you loved was strong but because you didn't act on it, eventually in time you gave up on it, losing the little bit you had left of the joy. Do you see where I am going with this? If you do not take action and invest in your joy, in time you will resign yourself to the fact that you cant experience it and you will have lost it all. That's a very horrible feeling if you ask me. Unfortunately, this is very common; I know several people who always wanted to get a college degree, and they were fired up about it, but they let other issues get in their way and distract them, the desire always remained but they did not take the actions to fulfill it. In time, every one of them said the same thing "It's too late for me, I can't finish it now". You see what happened? That initial joy has become misery. They just lost the little they had.

This is important to me because at one point I was one of those people who wanted a degree and because of life's curve balls, I never thought I could get one. I did not want to handle all the classes and the uneasiness of being in a class of students who could be my children practically. But God nudged me to investigate legitimate accredited online schools and not only did I get the degree, I avoided all the negative situations I had associated with school. I had no excuses. All is not lost if you find yourself in this situation, thankfully, so long as you are still alive you can still fulfill your life and increase your joy. But you must take action now and be on the look out for nudges from God.

I want to end this chapter with an example of how God nudged me to add this chapter to the book. When I first read the Parable of the Talents the first thought that came to my mind was 'this is a great parable about taking action and would be an excellent addition to the book'. However, I quickly doubted whether it would be appropriate because it portrayed the Master as being angry and I felt maybe this will offend some people. So I gave up on the idea and was about to send this text for final proof and eventually to the printer. But it wasn't meant to be, this chapter had to be here. During a few hours of downtime, I decided to read Dan Miller's 'No More Mondays'. Which is a great book and I highly recommend it. About 1/3 of the way through, Dan used the Parable of the Talents to say almost the exact same thing that I was thinking of saying in this book. I mean what are the odds of that happening? I was in turmoil over this chapter and made the uneasy decision of omitting it, but God NUDGED me to put it in.

Do you see how God works? My inner dialogue said 'don't put it in' but a "chance" synchronistic event made it very clear I had to. If I had listened to the words in my head, you would not be reading this chapter right now. Have faith, keep your eyes and mind open to God's nudges, it may come in ways you could not possibly imagine.

Chapter 6: Don't Make Debt Your God

"… the borrower is the slave of the lender." --Proverbs 22:7

Read that quote again, "…the borrower is the slave of the lender." When I read that quote, I was completely taken back by its truth. Debt is a prison sentence. It truly is. I know this well, I have been in that prison several times. Actually, in some countries it is literally a prison sentence, Debtors prison still exists in some parts of the world, who knows, you may live in one of those countries. Debt is by far one of the worst prisons to be in because of its impact on the mind. If you have debt, does it not feel like you are a prisoner to it? We acquire debt on our own accord, the lender is simply fulfilling a request for credit and we pile on the debt. This prison sentence is the only kind we directly bring on ourselves without committing a crime. Of course not all debt is necessarily bad, there are exceptions, for example buying a house or a real asset. That debt converts, we hope, in time to an asset, but credit card debt does not convert into anything but a prison sentence.

That $300 pair of shoes or that splurge on DVD's has become your master. Of course if you can afford to pay it, that is another story. But for the most part if you let the credit revolve, that debt makes you worry and imprisons you.

When Jesus said a man cannot serve God and money, he was referring not only to greed and the blind pursuit of money, but also debt. Think about it. Often when we are in debt, where does our devotion go? Not to God, but to the Debt. We worry so much more about debt that it takes more energy and thought power from us, power we could be using to make our lives more fulfilled. With that said, the debt has become your god and every day that you pray to it, the more those prayers are answered and the answers compound daily.

I know that is a hard thing to hear and harder to think about, but it's true. If you are in debt, think about it right now. Are you making the minimum payments? How long is the prison sentence going to be until you pay it off? A few long years right? That does not feel good does it? You are not alone. Nevertheless, you are also not condemned to the debt either, not if you turn to God for guidance.

Before I go on I want to say that I am not going to give you tips on how to save money or how to spend it; I could probably write a separate book on how to spend money, overspending was one of the things that brought me down during my dark days. However, I will show you that with faith and perseverance, your debt can be erased. **I am not talking about managing your debt, managing your debt brings you more debt, we don't want to manage debt, we want to get rid of it.** Makes sense right? Faith is the only way that you can start to tackle this issue. If you have too much debt and your income is not enough to cover it, or is barely covering it, what you need is God's guidance, since in your current capacity you won't be able to deal with it on your own. Simply put, give your debt up to God and let him handle it. Use the Law of Attraction to manifest more money. Your faith will make it so.

You must also act on the internal nudges you get from God. It could be a drastic move sometimes, but remember, we often cannot see the broader picture. God may nudge you to consolidate the debt, which may seem like a negative event, but in broader context that could be the best thing to ever happen to you, it can clear the way for future prosperity. Many successful people have had to do that several times before they made it, learning a valuable lesson every time they did it.

Look at your financial situation and see what's best for you. Be mindful of God's Nudges.

I won't leave it there; I am going to show you that God helps those with debt and I said earlier, often he may require you to take risks. The pages that will follow will illustrate how God has helped people get out of their debts in the Bible. I will quote those entire passages and discuss them. Let us open our Bibles to the following chapters:

2 Kings 4: 1-7 "Now the wife of one of the sons of the prophets cried to Elisha, "Your servant my husband is dead, and you know that your servant feared the Lord, but the creditor has come to take my two children to be his slaves." And Elisha said to her, "What shall I do for you? Tell me; what have you in the house?" And she said, "Your servant has nothing in the house except a jar of oil." Then he said, "Go outside, borrow vessels from all your neighbors, empty vessels and not too few. Then go in and shut the door behind yourself and your sons and pour into all these vessels. And when one is full, set it aside." So she went from him and shut the door behind herself and her sons. And as she poured they brought the vessels to her. When the vessels were full, she said to her son, "Bring me another vessel." And he said to her, "There is not another." Then the oil stopped flowing. She came and told the man of God, and he said, "Go, sell the oil and pay your debts, and you and your sons can live on the rest."

This story touched me deeply. This poor woman had nothing, her husband is dead and the two remaining people in her life, her sons, were about to be enslaved to pay off the husbands debt. Imagine being faced with this situation. Think about this poor woman. She is poor and in debt, the debt isn't even her own. Her sons may be the only two that can work to bring food into the home, and they are about to be taken away.

This could have turned into a very sad story. Thankfully, God had other plans. Notice what Elisha told this woman to do. She only had a little oil, but through God's grace, it multiplied. However, God's grace was only one part of the equation; actually, the biggest part of this was the woman's faith. In her faith, she followed the instructions set forth by Elisha, it took great courage for the woman to go out and borrow these vessels, she was acquiring more debt, which is usually a risky proposition. But Elisha was clearly working on God's orders, knowing full well a miracle would occur.

In the end, because of her faith, not only was her debt repaid in full, she had extra oil for herself and her children. If she had so desired, she could have sold it all and had excess money for herself and her family. The moral of the story is Trust God and leave it all up to him. When God pushes you in a direction, and you get that intuitive nudge to do something, **DO IT**. That could be the idea you need to get yourself out of debt. It may even the idea that may make you financially prosperous

Here is another wonderful story illustrating God's ability to erase debt, the situation is not as dire as the woman's story, but it is a great example of the miracles that can happen.

2 Kings 6:1-7 "Now the sons of the prophets said to Elisha, "See, the place where we dwell under your charge is too small for us. Let us go to the Jordan and each of us get there a log, and let us make a place for us to dwell there." And he answered, "Go." Then one of them said, "Be pleased to go with your servants." And he answered, "I will go." So he went with them. And when they came to the Jordan, they cut down trees. But as one was felling a log, his axe head fell into the water, and he cried out, "Alas, my master! It was borrowed." Then the man of God said, "Where did it fall?" When he showed him the place, he cut off a stick and threw it in there

and made the iron float. And he said, "Take it up." So he reached out his hand and took it."

This is also a great story, this poor man; a servant using a borrowed axe head, drops it in the water and is now in debt, his weekly and perhaps monthly wage probably does not even cover the cost of the axe. During those days, most axes were made of Iron. It probably sank like a rock. So imagine the predicament he is in; now we have a metal that sinks, and a servant who is now in debt. It seems almost completely hopeless. But alas, because of faith, it was brought back out of the water and now the servant, when he finishes his work, can return it to its rightful owner and not be burdened with debt. I could not imagine a better ending.

These two stories should be an inspiration to you. Trust in God that he will settle your debts, you may not know how, but that is not your job. Like I said, you may need to tack drastic action, or you may be guided to get help. Leave that to God. When you see money flow in because of your faith, the only thing that will be compounding is the interest in your bank account.

I know that seems rather easy and I wish I could end this chapter with just those stories, but there are a few more issues we need to discuss about money and prosperity, very important ones that must be addressed in order to remove the blocks you may have about money.
What is money? Money is energy, it flows and circulates, it never dies, it comes into form and takes on different forms, such as a car, gold, a new house, food. Money converts to all these things, at least that is how we decided it should be based on what we hold to be of value. Money simply put, is a measurement of value. It alone is only a means to an end and not an end in itself. I want to ask you three critical questions and I want you to be as honest as you can be with yourself about this.

Your answers could be the key to why financial prosperity does not flow in your life.

1 Do you think money is dirty or ungodly?
2 Are rich people untrustworthy and conniving?
3 Does making money with a hobby you love cheapen it for you?

If you answered yes to any of these questions, you have a block to your prosperity. In fact, by answering yes to one of these questions, by default, you answer yes to all of them. Let me explain why this is.

If you answered yes to number 1, by default you are then saying that because money is dirty and ungodly, the rich are pedaling in dirty and ungodly pursuits since they have a lot of money. By thinking, this you are saying yes to question 2 as well. You are also dissociating money with the activities that you love to do. If you love them, you don't want to taint them with money, thus saying yes to question 3. Do you see where I am going with this? Can you see how this can be a huge impediment to financial prosperity?

I want to get deeper into this because I am sure this is at the root of almost all negative experiences we have had with money.

Let's deal with Question 1 again, assuming you answered yes; money is dirty or ungodly. If this is the belief you hold, you can never have money flow into your life because in your mind you have a negative association about money.

Why would you want money to flow into your life if money is so dirty and ungodly? I certainly would not want anything that I thought was ungodly or dirty in my life. But that would be too simplistic because we need money to survive in the world regardless whether it is dirty or not. In that case, perhaps it is not prosperity that you want but a day-to-day existence, just getting by. Does that sound like a joyful proposition to you? If your answer is no, I advise you to rethink your ideas about money. Money will flow easier into your life when you can change your associations that you have about it. This conflict, if not resolved, is placing a huge wall between you and money. God gave us freedom to choose, but if you ask for one thing and feel resistance to it at the same time, he won't answer the prayer since you are not exercising your freedom of choice. **Ask and it shall be given to you.**

Question 2: Let's assume you answered yes to that one: Rich people are untrustworthy and conniving. Even if you answered no to question 1, by answering yes to question 2, you are answering yes to question 1 as well and you are giving God conflicting information again. Here is why: On the one hand, rich people are untrustworthy, but on the other, you want to be a rich person yourself. How can that be reconciled? It can't, it is another wall built to separate you from financial prosperity.

If rich people are untrustworthy, why would you want to be rich? That would mean you want to be untrustworthy and conniving and I know that's not what you want to be. If you say, 'I am a different kind of person, money won't corrupt me' then what you are saying is that it is not the money that is corrupting a person, but the persons own inclination to be corrupted by money. You see what I mean?

If you recall at the beginning of the book, I mentioned several people from the Bible who were rich beyond belief, how does the idea that rich people are untrustworthy and conniving fit within the context of their lives? Should

I dare say what answering yes to questions 1 or 2 would infer about those people of God? Do you see where I am going with this? I can hear you saying, "But Doron, these people were chosen by God, it doesn't apply to them"

Ahhh very good, well, I agree, God chose them. But did they know they were chosen before God made it known to them? No, they had no clue.

We have established earlier that nothing in this universe is random, that means you are not random either. God put you on this earth for a purpose right?

God doesn't waste time. Some might say "Doron, I am too old and do not have any skills, I do not have a purpose, my time has passed"

I wonder what would be of this world if Moses, the rock of the Old Testament had gotten away with those excuses. Do you remember the story of Moses? Did he know his purpose before God revealed himself to him? No, he had no clue. How old was Moses when God chose him and what excuse did Moses use to avoid God's purpose?

Let's find out: Please open the Bible to Exodus 4:10-12 "**And Moses said to the Lord, O Lord, I am not a man of words; I have never been so, and am not now, even after what you have said to your servant: for talking is hard for me, and I am slow of tongue. The LORD said to him, "Who has made man's mouth? Or who makes him mute or deaf, or seeing or blind? Is it not I, the LORD? "Now then go, and I, even I, will be with your mouth, and teach you what you are to say."**

God did not let Moses off the hook with his excuses, when God has a purpose for you, no matter how great or small, you will find it out at any age. **IF YOU ARE ALIVE, YOU ARE CHOSEN.**

Eventually when Moses went back to Egypt to free the Israelites from Bondage, how old was he?
Exodus 7:7" **Moses was eighty years old** and Aaron eighty-three, when they spoke to Pharaoh."

Everything is possible for God, it does not matter what age you are, you have a purpose. Moses of course was not the only one in the Bible who had excuses for God, Abraham and Sarah thought they were too old to have children, but they did. I could write an entire book about people in the Bible who gave God excuses but overcame every one of them. When we trust in God, excuses are just idle words; they are a hidden device of the Golden Calf.

This year (2009) is a sad time financially for the world and I don't mean just because so many people are suffering, that is also sad. But because of the extensive ideological damage it is causing. If you turn on the television, all you see are the rich people who ruined the entire world's economy because they were greedy. This inspires hatred.

Anyone could easily turn around and say, you see? 'Rich people are untrustworthy and conniving'. That might be true for some of them, but not all of them. We cannot condemn all rich people because a handful of greedy individuals damaged the world economy.
We must resist this notion as best we can because it will activate the Law of Attraction to bring more poverty to the world. We need to change our focus and realize that it is not money that is making a person untrustworthy or conniving, money is simply a tool. **Money enhances the type of person that you already are. If you have a charitable nature, money will make you more charitable, if you are stingy, money will make you stingier. Money is a tool of expression and like a car, it is pure utility, a car can save your life when you need to rush to a hospital, but a car**

can also be the reason you are going to the hospital in the first place. **Money has the same nature; it is how you use it, not its intrinsic nature.**

To attract money we need to clean up our thinking about money. We have to realize that criminals exist when there is too much money and when there is too little money. There is little difference between white-collar crime and blue-collar crime, the only difference is the sum of money involved and the particular status that person holds in society.

If you do not think about it critically and spiritually, it can be easy to fall under the sway of greed or desperation, but that's not moneys fault, but the person's negative ideas about money.

In short, both people who have money and those who don't are equally capable of doing bad things. This further illustrates money is only a tool; how you use it will determine its nature. Money is not evil and people who have it are only acting wrongly if they use it for evil. Now that you are armed with this knowledge, you can reframe money in your mind and let it flow in your life. If you consider yourself to be a good person money will only enhance your nature.

Now if you answered yes to question 3: That money would cheapen your experience of your hobby, then by default questions 1 and 2 would be yes as well. Answering yes to question 3 suggests that money has a cheapening and corrupting power, thus people who pursue it are cheapened and corrupted by it. As I illustrated above, money is only a tool and enhances a person's qualities, it doesn't cheapen the experience if you do not view it as such. There is however, a much deeper issue involved with answering yes to question 3.

Throughout my life and perhaps throughout your own, I have desired work that had meaning, work I could enjoy. If I am going to spend 8 hours a day at it, I would hope it would be enjoyable. Unfortunately, that is not the experience I had and probably not the experience for most people. I had mornings when I cried my way to work because I was so miserable. I went in, suffering the work saying to myself "I have to work so I can pay the bills, I don't have to like it, but I have to do it". That's a sad state of affairs isn't it? Waking up that miserable is horrible. What if I told you that doesn't have to be your reality? Would you believe me? Well, I am telling you …It doesn't have to be your reality.

Let's list a few things that we would hope we could experience at work.

1. Flexibility and freedom.
2. A sense of purpose and enjoyment.
3. A decent wage.

Those are all great qualities. It would be ideal if you could find a job like that. It would be paradise; in fact, if you had all those qualities in a job, you would be more than happy to work on weekends as well, right?

Let's make another list of the experiences you have with your hobbies:
1. Flexibility and freedom, you can practice your hobby when you choose.
2. A sense of purpose and enjoyment: Actively pursing your hobby gives you a sense of purpose and enjoyment.

I am sure there are many other reasons you enjoy your hobby. What is missing from this list? There isn't an income potential listed there. My question to you is: **Why isn't it listed there?** If you could have all the great qualities of work and an income as well, why don't you make your hobby into your work? As Mark Twain said **"Make your vocation, your vacation"**.

Imagine being able to make money and have all the great feelings associated with your hobby as well. It sounds almost too good to be true. But it can be done. With the advent of the internet, almost every hobby imaginable can be made into a business. Millions of people have the same hobby and would be willing to do business with you. But until you clean up your conception of money the above ideal scenario cannot be yours.

I urge you to take time and think about everything I wrote here. If you do not have a hobby you are passionate about, ask God for guidance. You can be happy and prosperous. God wants that for you, but only if you want it for yourself.

Deuteronomy 8:18: "…thou shalt remember the LORD your God, for it is **He that giveth thee power to get wealth**, that He may establish His covenant which He sware unto your fathers, as it is this day"

Chapter 7: What is Prosperity?

Is prosperity really only about money? When we ask ourselves 'what is prosperity?' We probably think about money. That's the first thing that used to come up in my mind. In fact that is the traditional definition of what prosperity is for most people. Prosperity always equals financial abundance in our society. As I have learned through my experiences in life, prosperity is not only about money, it is about health, spiritual and mental well-being as well.

You could win the lottery tomorrow but be dying of a disease. If you had a choice, what would you do? Take the chance that you would be relieved of the suffering and have your life spared? Or, take the money? I have a feeling I know the answer to that question. The answer you give will indicate to you that money alone is not prosperity. When you catch a bad cold or flu, did you even care about money? No, you were focused on getting better. Your life experiences alone can be a perfect example of this.

Take a look at the world's pop culture icons. They have so much money; they possess large houses, cars with gold plated hoods and rims. However, take a deeper look and tell me what else you see. You see tragic lives.

No matter how hard they try, they cannot buy themselves a new life. They are stuck in their minds, and those minds are prisons, and they are often serving life sentences. They don't have prosperity, they just have money. Lose your mind and soul and all the money in the world won't get them back.

If you get anything out of this chapter, please understand those who have only money are not to be envied, you probably have a much better quality of life than they do. Fine, maybe they have a better car or home and flashier clothing, but when you go to sleep at night, will all that money take the pain away? No, it can bury the pain, but **what you bury alive never dies**. **It will pop up again and in much more painful ways.**

"It's good to have money and the things that money can buy, but it's good, too, to check up once in a while and make sure that you haven't lost the things that money can't buy. " ~George Horace Lorimer

Isn't that a remarkable quote? Unfortunately, for our pop culture friends, they are losing or have lost the things money can't buy. Therefore, please do not be envious. You are very prosperous in comparison. Really, you are, don't doubt that for a moment.

I will give you a quick insight into how I realized prosperity was more than money. At points in my life, I had inherited money of various amounts. I believed I had it all and that the money would make my life better. But what did I do? I spent it all, and because I had money to live, I became complacent and bored. I would drink and spend wildly. Sound familiar? The Same thing the pop icons are doing, although I did not inherit a fraction of what they have, the result was the same.

The reason I did not have prosperity was because I was not whole. Prosperity is about being whole in all parts of your life. Oh and by the way, every dollar of that money I inherited has been spent. I had even gotten into debt several times and had to go bankrupt as I mentioned in a previous chapter. That's not prosperity if you ask me. One thing I had that kept me from ending up like these pop icons was faith in God and even the little faith I had, protected me from the awful fate some of these people are going through. I had to make the same mistake again and again to understand that prosperity involves all areas of life not just in one area.

As it states in 3 John Verse 2 "Beloved I wish above all things that **thou mayest prosper and be in health, even as thy soul prospers**."

The key words here are "prosper" and "health" he is addressing physical prosperity here.
He says prosper and be in good health. If by prosper, he meant just money he would not have mentioned health as well. He is saying prosperity in all of your life. However, he did have a qualifier, "even as your soul prospers"

He is saying you need to be in alignment with God's Law of Attraction to get prosperous. You see folks; The Bible is clear on this, if poverty was the only way one was to be in God's good graces, prosperity would not be mentioned and there wouldn't be Godly people in the Bible with money and happiness. Although there is a quote in the Bible that states the love of money is the root of all evil. It can be, as I explained in a previous chapter, but only when it is used in the spirit of greed. That quote only applies to greed. The pursuit of money alone could be the root of all evil, but with a whole and happy person, it is the root of much good.

Chapter 8: Stories of Faith

The Bible is packed with stories of how faith has changed outcomes to major events through time. If you think about it, if it were not for the events in the Bible, most of Western civilization would not exist. Think about that for a moment. What would have happened if Moses was allowed to get away with his excuses? He would have never led the Israelite's out of Egypt. If the Israelites were not set free, then Judaism would not have been, the Israelite's overtime would have melted into Egyptian and Babylonian cultures and there would be no Biblical tradition at all. No Christianity, no Judaism. Without the Biblical tradition where would America be? Where would the world be? Where would you be? Interesting questions to ponder. Although my reason for illustrating stories of faith is to illustrate how the core of the Law of Attraction is faith and of letting go and letting God, I want you to also imagine how significant these stories are and why having faith can change the world, starting with one person at a time. Starting with you.

Your faith in divine providence can turn you into a tool for God's work, but only if you declare and have faith that God will give you abundance. Who knows what abundance will allow you to do? The possibilities are endless.

We are going to examine two stories of faith from the Bible and how that faith brought about great things for those who held fast to it and attracted redemption and prosperity.

Hannah prays in faith to have a child, and she was given a child. We will examine the story of Joseph and how he was sold into slavery, but because of his faith in God, not only did he become great personally, but his story is a cornerstone in the Biblical tradition. More importantly, it illustrates that when you simply let go, the divine plan becomes apparent.

As I said in a previous chapter, sometimes we do not understand God's plan for our lives.

Hannah's Prayer:

1 Samuel Chapters 1-2

If you open the Bible up to the first book of Samuel, the story of Hannah can be found. This story does not only indicate God's great mercy but also his willingness to answer prayer

Hannah was one of two wives of Elkanah, of the two wives; she was the one who was unable to have children. There is no greater pain for a person if they want to have children, and they cannot, it is as if a part of them remains unfulfilled forever. The second wife Peninnah had children, and whenever she had a chance, she would flaunt that fact in Hannah's face. Hannah was miserable, and every time she was reminded, she would cry, lose her appetite and fall into a deep depression. She had finally had enough and realized at this point she had to get herself together and really be serious about her devotion to God and allow God to work through her. She went through a period of intensive prayer, devoting her full heart to God, so much so that she was believed to have been drunk, but she was not drunk, but engulfed in prayer to God. She had made a vow to consecrate the fruit of her womb to God. God is merciful; he granted her a son, and not just any son but the future King of Israel.

Her prayers were answered beyond her wildest dreams as she states in 1 Samuel 1:27 **"I prayed for this child and the Lord granted me what I asked of him"**
The element that ties this to the Law of Attraction is very direct, you must ask for what you want and believe in the power of God to make it so. As Jesus said **"Ask, and it shall be given unto you."** Have you asked?

Joseph's Story
God works in mysterious ways
Genesis 37-46

Joseph was the son of the great patriarch Jacob and his wife Rachel. Joseph was the most beloved son of Jacob. He was most beloved because he was born unto to Jacob when he was advanced in age. Jacob in his love for Joseph created a multicolored and ornamented robe for him. It was said that this robe was so rich in color and ornaments that it was an amazing sight. You have to understand that during Jacob's time, fabric that was ornamented or even dyed different colors was incredibly expensive; the dyes were not easy or cheap to make. Just imagine how wonderful and valuable this robe was. Jacob's favor came with a high price, Joseph's brothers saw that he had received such a robe from their father and they did not. This made them very jealous of Joseph. It didn't help that Joseph had a dream about his sheaves of grain and how it would surpass his brothers.

This dream only served to inspire more hatred for Joseph in the eyes of his brothers. The following day he has another dream that further incited them. One wonders what Joseph's intentions were when he kept on provoking his brothers' hatred. Could it be because he was a teenager and wanted to be a bit rambunctious? I am not so sure. Often we do things that seem counter to what we should be doing. However, in reality, it is God's work and it all makes sense in the course of time.

The adage 'God works in mysterious ways' is true, not only in your life but throughout history and especially in the story of Joseph.

After these dreams, the brothers' hatred grew, so much so that even his father Jacob was concerned and rebuked the young Joseph about the dreams, but decided afterwards to let the matter go. One day as the brothers were grazing the flock, Joseph went out to meet them. They saw him coming and were plotting to kill him and throw him in cistern so the animals could come and devour him. Not every brother was willing to kill him; Reuben was the only voice of reason.

So Joseph meets them in the field, the brothers' strip him of his robe, and throw him in a cistern. The cistern was empty at the time. The brothers then see a caravan of Ishmaelite traders and eventually sell him to them. They took the robe and dipped it in the blood of a slaughtered goat so it would appear that an animal killed Joseph. They presented this to their father Jacob, he noticed it was Joseph's robe and there was blood on it. He was convinced Joseph was dead and mourned greatly for his loss.

The Ishmaelite's went on to sell Joseph to Egypt as a servant. This would turn out to be a very good thing for Joseph in the end. As it states in the Genesis 39: 2-3 "2 **The LORD was with Joseph, and he prospered, and he lived-in the household of his Egyptian master. 3 When his master saw that the LORD was with him and that the LORD generously gave him success in everything he did.**" In another twist of fate as Joseph was prospering and was becoming close to the upper-echelons of Ancient Egypt, he was embroiled in a scandal and was sent to prison for some time. Again, God would work in mysterious ways. Time passes and while in prison, Pharaoh had dreams, and it so happened Joseph had a reputation for interpreting dreams accurately. He was called on to interpret them.

The dream Pharaoh had was dire, it foretold of an impending famine that would occur, luckily this dream served as warning to Pharaoh that something had to be done fast or Egypt would be swallowed by famine and would disappear in the sands of time.

Due to Joseph's dream interpreting skills; Pharaoh had left the entire land and fate of the Egyptians to Joseph and put him in control of the granaries and the economy of Egypt. What a huge responsibility that had to be. As you may have imagined, he made Egypt prosper and eventually people all across the Middle East were knocking on his borders to get some grain. Thanks to Joseph, Egypt was the only country with an abundance of grain to spare.

The famine was widespread, Joseph's family was no exception, they were hit with famine as well, and they needed food, so his brothers were sent to Egypt to buy grain. Several years had passed from the time Joseph was sold to the Egyptians to the time of the famine. When his brothers arrived he immediately recognized them, but they did not recognize him. Eventually, as time goes by he does reveal himself to his brothers and eventually his family, including his father move to Egypt and settle there since the food was in good supply.

They prospered there at least until a little after Joseph died. All in all a happy ending to that part of the story.

Think about this story for a moment, if it were not for this event, we would not have a western tradition; the Israelites would not have had an Exodus.

The reason I mentioned this story may not seem so obvious at first. But if you read through the chapters that describe Joseph's adventures, he never once complained or doubted. That's a lesson, he simply let go and let God, his faith was so strong that God would take care of him; he never complained about it, he knew he would be all right and he was. **Adversity almost always leads to opportunity.**

Have faith in God's ability to work in your life, it may not make sense all the time, but trust that it is the right thing for you. You may think I am stretching it, but you will see that Joseph's uprightness as a person and his self-assuredness made him so adored in God's sight, he ended up not only personally prospering, but we owe much of our spiritual and intellectual traditions to his life. The best phrase I can use to sum up this story is 'God works in mysterious ways'. Think about it.

When something bad happens to you, and you don't know the meaning, it is God working in mysterious ways.

Both these stories illustrate what you must do to activate God's Law of Attraction. Ask and be assured of its outcome and then let go and let God. I could have taken so many other stories of faith from the Biblo, but I believe the best thing for you to do is go through the Bible and find the particular stories that will motivate you. I really love the story of Joseph and Hannah, they both touch me deeply. Find a story in the Bible of faith and fashion your life by it and you will see that God will grant you through the Law of Attraction what you need and oftentimes, even better than you had ever imagined. God bless.

Chapter 9: Showing Gratitude

No matter where you may be in your life right now; whether it is a place you always wanted to be in, or perhaps you are going through a dark moment in your life. It will always help you to be grateful to God for everything you already have. This is a concept covered in all the other books on the Law of Attraction, and for good reason. Gratitude is of the highest importance. I want you to think right now; in fact take out a pen and write down what you have to be thankful for. (Sorry, one more exercise). If you say you have nothing to be thankful for, I would ask you to think again. Everything you have taken for granted is a reason to be thankful for. For example, are you reading this? Or having it read to you? Can you see it? Hear it? If so, is that not a remarkable gift? So many people in the world cannot see or hear anything, yet they are alive and many live robust lives.

Have you heard something that made you laugh? That's an amazing gift. Laughter is food for the soul. Be thankful you can laugh despite all the heartaches you may be going through or have gone through. I can go on and on with a list of things you should be grateful for without even knowing you.

Only you know what it is that you need to be grateful for. Look around you; I don't care if you live in a shelter or a rundown home. Do you have to sleep in the cold? Did you have the money to buy this book? Or did someone give it to you? Does it matter? You are here reading it right now. That's an amazing gift. Do this exercise with me. Write down a few things that you are grateful to God for. Write this out:

I thank you Lord for :

_____
_____
_____
_____
_____

_____ Praise God, for you are the source of all blessings in my life. Thank you. Amen

Write as much as you can, even write the little things that happon to you daily that are cause for gratitude. I don't care how small or large it is. God created all things, little things mean so much as well. I will end this chapter with a great quote, which sums up the chapter rather well.

"If the only prayer you ever say in your whole life is "thank you," that would suffice."--Meister Eckhart.

Chapter 10: Prayers

"God answers sharp and sudden on some prayers, and thrusts the thing we have prayed for in our face, A gauntlet with a gift in't. Every wish is like a prayer...with God"--Elizabeth Browning "Aurora Leigh"

This is technically not a full chapter, but I am taking time here to pray with you. Take a few moments and let's spend this quiet time letting God know your desires and how grateful you are for his abundance. You can alter the prayers however you like or you can use your own. These are the ones I use in my life, and I hope if anything, they will give you a new perspective in prayer.

Prayer of Gratitude:

Lord God, thank you for this quiet moment, this quiet moment where I can commune with you. As I think back through my life, I have seen you work miracles for me. From the first breath I took, to the food that you supply me for my nourishment and for all the people in my life, even those who I perceive to have done me wrong, I want to thank you for all of these things. I know that sometimes I need to go through some hard times to get to the good times. Thank you for the ability and opportunity to grow.

I know that no matter how far I feel that I have strayed from your presence, I know you still love me. The pain and anguish I feel are messengers of your love, you love me so much that you are willing to shift the universe to wake me up. Thank you for that. I know I am one of many billions of people in the world, but you have told us through your holy books that each one of us is special and each one of us is to face you when the time has come. Thank you so much for that opportunity to glance at your face and for the ways and means to fulfill our souls desire to be in your presence. Thank you.

Prayer for the Fulfillment of Goals:

Blessed God, I commune today not because you need to hear this, for you know what I need and want in my life, but as it is written in your book. "Ask and you shall receive". I am asking, God in full faith that you will answer me with the fulfillment of my desire or something better. I ask you in your infinite power that _____ be a reality in my life. At this point in my life, I feel and intend for this to be in my reality. I am allowing myself to feel and receive your guidance on this matter, I ask that you bring all people, events and circumstances together to create and manifest my desire. I know in faith that you will fulfill this desire and that if it turns out that my desire is not good for me, your will be done. I will look every day for the signs of the fulfillment and record them. I know that you hear my prayers, and I ask in faith that this desire or something better come to me. Thank you Lord God. Amen.

Prayer for Faith:

Merciful God and creator of all there was, is and ever will be, I pray to you for faith. Sometimes it is hard for me to keep my faith. With the turmoil in the world and in my life, I often feel the bitterness of doubt and my mind is so willing to build a golden calf. But I know better God. I ask for your help in keeping the fire of faith burning strongly for you Lord. As it states in Mark 9:24 '"Lord, I believe; help though my unbelief." Help me overcome the vestiges of doubt in me. Let me not stray as the Israelites did when Moses was on your mountain, lead me not into temptation but deliver me in faith. Thank you God, I love you. Amen.

These prayers give me great solace in my life, and I hope you can use them and change them to your liking. Prayer is a personal matter, what feels right for one person may not feel right for another, but one thing must be present and that's faith, it doesn't matter how you pray. Do you believe it can be a reality? If so, what you desire is coming to you without delay, faster than you can imagine.

Conclusion

I want to thank you again for buying this book, my goal was to get the word out there for those who wanted a quick reference and understanding of the Law of Attraction as it pertains to the Bible. I will suggest one thing that will help you immensely and that is to buy a notebook and keep it as your Law of Attraction Journal. Write your desires there, write your prayers and thoughts and date them, because I know if you keep the faith, in one years' time you will look back at the early entries and see just how much of what you desired came to be.

Any notebook will do. Keep it a secret; thoughts which only you and God will share. God is not only your creator, but he is your closest friend and adviser. God has a symbiotic relationship with you. You and God are a team. He will work through you, but you must have faith that he is there to help. As it says in the Psalms 90:17 "Let the favor of the Lord our God be on us; establish the work of our hands for us; yes, establish the work of our hands."

He will not only establish your work, but he will work through you to gain the best that life has to offer. Do you believe this is so?

About the Author

Doron Alon is the author of 48 books, owner of the publishing company Numinosity Press Inc.

For the last four years, Doron has dedicated every waking moment to designing Spiritual Techniques that help people break through their limitations to achieve success and inner peace in their lives..

Doron's background and 25 years of experience in meditation training, Meridian tapping (also known as E.F.T), Subliminal Messaging, Law of Attraction and more has helped him to focus on the techniques that provide the best results, and collate them for you in an easy to understand format. He is also a history buff and kindle publishing expert and will be releasing books in that genre as well.

More Books in this genre By Doron:

http://www.amazon.com/author/doronalon

God is in the Whispering

As I randomly opened the Old Testament. I opened to the first chapter that I stumbled upon. I opened to the story of Elijah. At first glance, it is a little adventure, lots of drama. Elijah is on the run after killing the 400 priests of Baal. Jezebel wanted to kill him. But a paragraph arrested me; it's a paragraph I have read countless times in my study of the Bible. After reading it, its profundity smacked right into me, it was as if I slammed into a wall and 20 years of study was summed up in one moment.

Here is the passage.

1 Kings 11 The LORD said, "Go out and stand on the mountain in the presence of the LORD , for the LORD is about to pass by." Then a great and powerful wind tore the mountains apart and shattered the rocks before the LORD , but the LORD was not in the wind. After the wind there was an earthquake, but the LORD was not in the earthquake. 12 After the earthquake came a fire, but the LORD was not in the fire. And after the fire came a gentle whisper. 13 When Elijah heard it, he pulled his cloak over his face and went out and stood at the mouth of the cave"

   In all those extreme examples of strength, God was not in them. God was in the whisper, this is a very important point. This passage is telling us that God also appears in the whisper and the subtle. It's a whisper we can't hear because we are searching for God in the noise. Listen, turn off. Just a gentle whisper.

Select Verses about the Law of Attraction

Matthew 7:7 "Ask and it will be given to you; seek and you will find; knock and the door will be opened to you."

Proverbs 23:7 "It is through thinking that man forms that which he is."

John 14:12 "I tell you the truth, anyone who has faith in me will do what I have been doing. He will do even greater things than these."

Matthew 21:22 "Whatsoever ye shall ask in prayer, believing, ye shall receive."

Mark 11:24 "What things soever ye desire, When ye pray, believe that ye receive them, and ye shall have them."

Matthew 8: 5-13 "when Jesus had entered Capernaum, a centurion came to him, asking for help. "Lord," he said, "my servant lies at home paralyzed and in terrible suffering." Jesus said to him, "I will go and heal him." The centurion replied, "Lord, I do not deserve to have you come under my roof. But just say the word, and my servant will be healed. For I myself am a man under authority, with soldiers under me. I tell this one, 'Go,' and he goes; and that one, 'Come,' and he comes. I say to my servant, 'Do this,' and he does it." When Jesus heard this, he was astonished and said to those following him, "I tell you the truth, I have not found anyone in Israel with such great faith. I say to you that many will come from the east and the west, and will take their places at the feast with Abraham, Isaac and Jacob in the kingdom of heaven. But the subjects of the kingdom will be thrown outside, into the darkness, where there will be weeping and gnashing of teeth." Then Jesus said to the centurion, "Go! It will be done just as you believed it would." And his servant was healed at that very hour."

Matthew 9:20-22 " Just then a woman who had been subject to bleeding for twelve years came up behind him and touched the edge of his cloak. She said to herself, "If I only touch his cloak, I will be healed." Jesus turned and saw her. "Take heart, daughter," he said, "your faith has healed you." And the woman was healed from that moment."

Matthew 9:27-29 it states " As Jesus went on from there, two blind men followed him, calling out, "Have mercy on us, Son of David!" When he had gone indoors, the blind men came to him, and he asked them, "Do you believe I can do this?" "Yes, Lord," they replied. Then he touched their eyes and said, "According to your faith will it be done to you"; and their sight was restored."

Matthew 17:20 "I tell you the truth, if you have faith as small as a mustard seed, you can say to this mountain, 'Move from here to there' and it will move. Nothing will be impossible for you."

Mark 9:23 "All things are possible to him that believes."

John 20:29 "Blessed are they that have not seen, and yet believe."

Hebrews 11:1 "Faith is the substance of things hoped for, the evidence of things not seen"

James 4: 2-3 "Ye Lust and have not: ye kill, and desire to have, and cannot obtain: ye fight and war, yet ye have not, because ye ask not. Ye ask and receive not because ye ask amiss."

John 20:29 "Blessed are they that have not seen, and yet believe"

Psalms 90:17 "Let the favor of the Lord our God be on us; establish the work of our hands for us; yes, establish the work of our hands."